The Ig

By Carmie Ruiz   **Illustrated by Sheila Bailey**

Target Skill Short *Ii*/i/

Scott Foresman
is an imprint of

PEARSON

iguana

We have a little iguana.

igloo

4

We have a little igloo.

It is for the little iguana.

He likes the little igloo.

We like the little iguana.